BIBLE CHARACTERS FOR
ADVENT
The Stories That Brought Us Christmas

Written and Illustrated by
THERESA & CHARLES POBEE-MENSAH

for Charlie
our Advent baby

For the FREE ebook and more, visit
www.BibleCharactersForAdvent.com

Nihil Obstat: Reverend James M. Dunfee, Censor Librorum
Imprimatur: Most Reverend Jeffrey M. Monforton, Bishop, Diocese of Steubenville.

Table of Contents

Introduction

God created man to know Him, love Him and serve Him, so that we could be happy with Him in heaven.

In the Bible, God made covenants with His people so they could become His children.

A covenant is a special promise between two people that makes them family.

A husband and wife make a covenant with each other when they get married. They promise to love each other, and they become one family.

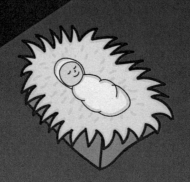

God sent His son, Jesus, into the world to make a covenant that would last forever.

Jesus did this by dying on the cross. Now all people can be children of God and go to heaven.

How To Read This Book

In this book, there are twenty-five characters that lead to Christmas. You can read one each day starting on December first, or you can read a few at a time.

1. GOD THE FATHER

This is the story of everything that happened from the beginning of time until Jesus was born in Bethlehem on Christmas Day.

A long, long time ago, God created the world from nothing.

On the first day, God separated the light from the darkness. This is when time began. It was the first day.

On the second day, God separated the sea from the sky. This made the space that God would fill with wonderful creatures.

On the third day, God made beautiful land covered with trees, flowers and grass.

On the fourth day, God created the sun, the moon and the stars to keep track of time.

On the fifth day, God created all different kinds of fish to fill the sea and birds to fill the sky.

On the sixth day, God created all the animals, large and small, to fill the land.

Then God created the most special thing of all. God created man in His image and likeness.

The Story of Creation - Genesis 1:1

On the seventh day, God rested. He was very happy with everything He made.

God loved everything He made so much that one day, many years later, He sent His only Son, Jesus, to the world on Christmas Day.

2. Adam & Eve

When God created the world, He made a covenant with Adam, the first man. Adam promised to obey God, and God promised to bless Adam and make him His son. God gave Adam a beautiful place to live called the Garden of Eden.

Even with all the animals Adam was lonely, so God created Eve to be Adam's wife.

God gave Adam and Eve many beautiful things to enjoy in the Garden of Eden. There was only one rule. They were not allowed to eat the fruit from the tree in the center of the garden.

The devil disguised himself as a snake and tempted them. Sadly, Adam and Eve disobeyed God and broke their covenant. Because they did not listen to God, Adam and Eve had to leave the Garden of Eden.

Life was much harder outside the garden, but God promised to send His son, Jesus. Jesus came so that we may all go to heaven.

The Fall of Man - *Genesis 3:1*

3. Seth

When Adam and Eve began their life outside the Garden of Eden, they were sad to be away from God and all the beautiful things.

They remembered that God wanted them to start a family. Seth was Adam and Eve's son.

The Bible tells us that Seth was made in the image and likeness of Adam, just like Adam was made in the image and likeness of God.

Seth in Adam's Image and Likeness - *Genesis 5:3*

Adam and Eve were the first parents of all the people in the world.

One of the things that makes people different from all of the other creatures on earth is that people are made in the image and likeness of God.

When Adam and Eve disobeyed God, all the people of the world were separated from Him.

God promised to send His son Jesus so we could all be His children.

4. NOAH

Noah is very important because God made His second covenant with him.

After Adam and Eve, the world was filled with people, but the people forgot about God's laws and did many bad things.

Noah's Ark - Genesis 6:14

God told Noah to build an Ark. While he was building the ark, Noah told the people to turn away from evil and follow God.

None of the people listened. Instead they just laughed at Noah. When the Ark was finished, Noah brought his family and two of every animal onto the ark.

God sent rain for forty days and forty nights. Finally, the Ark came to rest on top of a mountain. Noah and his family were safe.

When they came out of the ark, God made a covenant with Noah.

God promised that He would never again destroy the earth with a flood. Noah and his family promised to obey God's laws.

There was a beautiful rainbow in the sky as a sign of God's covenant with Noah.

5. SHEM

Shem was one of Noah's sons. Many people believe that Shem is also the great king Melchizedek. You say his name like this:

MEL - KEYS - A - DECK

Melchizedek was a priest and king in the Old Testament.

Most priests in the Old Testament would offer God sacrifices of animals.

Instead, Melchizedek offered God a sacrifice of bread and wine.

Melchizedek Offers Bread and Wine
Genesis 14:18

When Jesus came, people said that He was a priest like Melchizedek. At the last supper, Jesus gave us His body and blood under the appearance of bread and wine.

The Last Supper - Matthew 26:26

6. ABRAHAM

When Abraham was little, his name was Abram, but when he grew up God made a covenant with him and changed his name to Abraham.

God Promises to Bless Abraham - *Genesis 22:15*

In his covenant, God promised to bless Abraham's family. God blessed Abraham and Sarah with a son, Isaac. Isaac was Abraham and Sarah's only son just like Jesus was God's only Son.

When God made a covenant with Adam and Noah, all the people on earth were included. This time, God made a covenant with just Abraham's family.

God did not forget about all the other people in the world; instead, He promised to bless all the people of the world through Abraham's family.

This happened when Jesus came. Jesus was from Abraham's family, but Jesus came to save all people.

7. JACOB

Jacob was Isaac's son. Like Abraham, Jacob's name was changed too. Jacob's new name was Israel.

Israel had twelve sons and their families became known as the twelve tribes of Israel.

God's covenant with Abraham was passed on to the tribes of Israel, and they became God's people.

The twelve tribes of Israel became a great nation just like God promised Abraham.

Jacob Blesses His Sons - *Genesis 49:28*

When Jesus came, He picked twelve men to be His apostles and start His Church.

Jesus' followers grew from the twelve apostles to millions of people all over the world.

The Church is the new people of God just like the twelve tribes of Israel were the first people of God.

Jesus Calls the Apostles- Matthew 4:18

The Twelve Apostles - Matthew 10:2

8. JOSEPH

One of Jacob's sons was named Joseph. Joseph had a dream that he would rule over all his brothers. This made his brothers mad.

His brothers sold him to some travelers who were going to Egypt.

Joseph Is Sold Into Slavery
Genesis 37:28

When Pharaoh, the king of Egypt, saw how wise Joseph was, he let Joseph rule with him.

Then there was a great famine in all the land. This meant that no rain came for many, many days. It was very hard to find food.

Joseph's brothers traveled to Egypt to ask for food. When Joseph saw his brothers he forgave them.

Joseph invited all his brothers to move to Egypt with their families.

Joseph Forgives His Brothers - *Genesis 45:4*

This way there would be plenty of food for all of them.

Joseph reminds us of Jesus. When Jesus was on earth many people treated Him unkindly too, but Jesus always forgave them.

Jesus Is Betrayed - Luke 22:47

Jesus Appears to the Apostles - John 20:19

The Israelites kept living in Egypt for a long time. A new Pharaoh came who did not know Joseph and did not like the Israelites living in his land.

This Pharaoh was not nice to God's people. The Israelites prayed for God to save them. Next, we will see who God sent to save His people.

9. MOSES

God heard the Israelites' prayer. He sent Moses to lead His people out of Egypt to the Promised Land.

In the desert, God made a covenant with Moses and the Israelites. God gave Moses the Ten Commandments on two stone tablets, and the Israelites became the children of God.

The Ten Commandments - Exodus 20:1

Moses Parts the Red Sea - Exodus 14:16

The Bible tells us that one day, a prophet like Moses would come again.

It is talking about Jesus. Jesus, like Moses, spoke directly to God and performed many miracles.

A Prophet Like Moses Will Come - *Deuteronomy 18:15*

Jesus Walks on Water - *Matthew 14:25*

10. JOSHUA

After Moses died, Joshua became the Israelites' new leader.

It was a long journey to the Promised Land.

On the way, some of the people decided not to listen to God. Because they would not listen, they could not enter the Promised Land for a long time.

God Appoints Joshua - Joshua 1:1

The Israelites Cross the Jordan - *Joshua 3:14*

Finally, after forty years, Joshua led the Israelites out of the desert and into the Promised Land.

Joshua reminds us of Jesus. Jesus leads us from earth to our heavenly home, just like Joshua led the Israelites to the Promised Land.

II. Rahab

Rahab lived in the Promised Land, but Rahab was not an Israelite.

When the Israelites arrived they needed help getting into the Promised Land. Joshua sent spies into the city.

The leaders of the city were mad. They sent soldiers to find the spies.

Rahab hid the spies on the roof of her house so the soldiers would not find them. Rahab saved their lives!

Later, when the Israelites took over the Promised Land they told Rahab to hang a red cord in her window.

The red chord meant that the Israelites should not take over her house.

Rahab Is Saved - *Joshua 2:18*

The red chord reminds us of Jesus who saved us with His blood when He died on the cross.

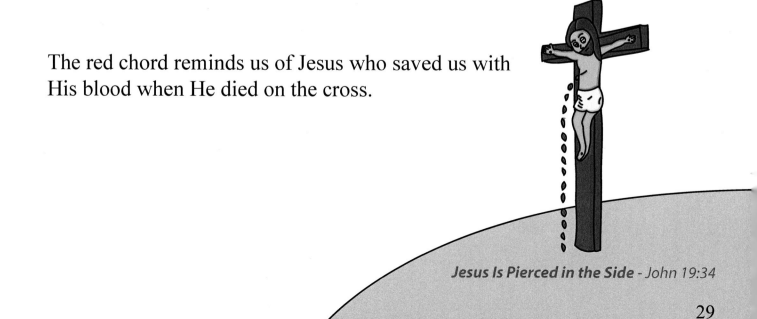

Jesus Is Pierced in the Side - *John 19:34*

29

12. Samson

Samson was stronger than any man. He helped the Israelites when they were attacked by the Philistines.

Samson promised God that he would never cut his hair. This was the secret to his incredible strength.

Samson Slays A Thousand Men - *Judges 15:15*

One day, the Philistines tricked Samson into telling his secret. His hair was cut, and he lost his strength. Then, the Philistines captured him.

After Samson's hair grew back, he prayed to God saying that he was sorry. God gave him his strength back.

Samson defeated the Philistines by crashing down a building on them, and the Israelites were saved.

Samson Destroys the Philistines' Temple - *Judges 16:28*

31

13. Ruth

Ruth and Naomi went on a journey to the Promised Land.

Ruth wanted a husband who was an Israelite so they could raise a family to worship God.

It was a beautiful love story. She met a man named Boaz and they were married.

Even though Ruth was not an Israelite, she was welcomed to worship the true God.

Ruth and Boaz became the great-grandparents of the powerful King David.

Ruth Meets Boaz - Ruth 2:1

In the Bible, Jesus preached the gospel to all people. Ruth reminds us of this because she was welcomed to worship God even though she was not an Israelite.

14. JESSE

Jesse had many sons. His youngest son, David, was anointed as the king of all of Israel.

Before David was anointed king, he was a shepherd and took care of his family's sheep.

David Tends Jesse's Sheep - 1 Samual 17:15

The Bible tells us that Jesus will come from Jesse's family. Jesus is like Jesse's son, David, in many ways.

Just like David, Jesus was a shepherd. But instead of sheep, Jesus watches over all of us.

Jesus Is the Good Shephard - *John 10:11*

15. David

After being anointed by Samuel, David became the great king of Israel. David was the first good king to rule over Israel, and is the most important king in the Old Testament.

David Wants to Build a Temple - *2 Samuel 7:1*

David made plans to build a beautiful temple for all the Israelites to worship God.

The Bible called Jesus the son of David. Like David, Jesus is a great king who rules over God's people.

Jesus Is Called Son of David - *Matthew 20:30*

Jesus Is Crowned with Power and Glory - *Luke 21:27*

When God made a covenant with David, it was very special. David promised that the Israelites would obey all God's laws and God promised to bless the Israelites and make them His people.

This was the last covenant that God made before Jesus came.

37

16. SOLOMON

Solomon was King David's son. When he became king, God told him that he could ask for any gift.

Instead of asking for riches, power, or a long life, Solomon asked for wisdom so he could be a good ruler of God's people.

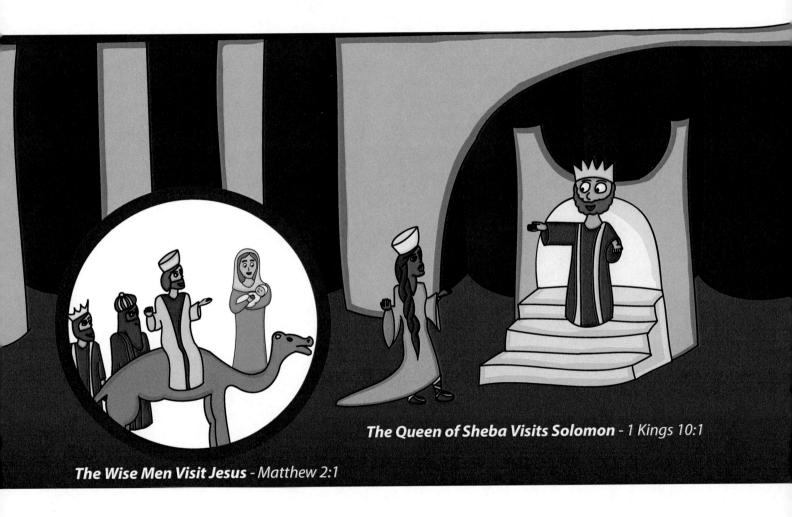

The Wise Men Visit Jesus - Matthew 2:1

The Queen of Sheba Visits Solomon - 1 Kings 10:1

God blessed Solomon with great wisdom and people from all the lands came to hear him. This reminds us of the three wise men who traveled from faraway lands to see Jesus.

Solomon built the temple that his father, King David, wanted. This was a beautiful place for God's people to pray.

With all his wisdom Solomon became very rich and powerful.

Solomon Builds the Temple - 1 Kings 6:14

Sadly, he forgot that God gave him his wisdom and he turned away from God.

When Jesus came, even though He was tempted by the devil, He always obeyed God. So, unlike Solomon, Jesus is the perfect, wise king.

17. Elijah

God's people continued to forget about their covenant with Him. God sent another prophet, Elijah, who performed many miracles for the people.

Elijah also reminded the people to turn away from sin and follow God.

Elijah Calls Fire from Heaven - *2 Kings 1:10*

Like Elijah, Jesus performed many miracles and reminded people to turn their lives back to God.

Jesus Turns Water into Wine- John 2:1

18. Jeroboam & Rehoboam

The Israelites all lived in one kingdom and Solomon was their king. After Solomon disobeyed God, the kingdom was split into two kingdoms.

The Kingdom of Israel Splits - 1 Kings 12:16

Jeroboam was the king of the Northern Kingdom. The people in Jeroboam's kingdom married people who did not worship God. Later they became part of the Gentiles.

The Gentiles were not the people of God, because God had not made a covenant with them yet.

Rehoboam was the king of the Southern Kingdom. All the people in Rehoboam's kingdom became known as the Jews because they were from the tribe of Judah.

This is important because Jesus was Jewish, meaning that He was from the southern kingdom and the tribe of Judah.

Jesus Tells the Disciples to Baptize People of All Nations - Matthew 28:19

When Jesus came He preached to the Jews and the Gentiles. Jesus brought both of the kingdoms back together.

19. Isaiah

Isaiah was a prophet when the kingdom was divided. He told the people if they did not start listening to God they would go into exile.

Exile meant they would be sent away from the Promised Land.

Sadly, the people did not listen to Isaiah and had to leave the Promised Land.

The Exile Is Foretold - Isaiah 5:13

Even though God's people continued to disobey, God still loved them.

Isaiah told the people that one day a child would be born who is the Prince of Peace. He was talking about Jesus.

Isaiah also told them about the New Covenant. The New Covenant is when Jesus came into the world to save all people by dying on the cross.

Isaiah Foretells Jesus' Birth - Isaiah 9:5

20. Jeremiah

Jeremiah was a priest and prophet while the Israelites were in exile.

Remember, exile means the Israelites were sent away from the Promised Land.

While the Israelites were in exile, the temple where the Israelites worshiped God was destroyed. This made Jeremiah sad.

The Temple Is Destroyed - 2 Kings 25:8

Even though the temple was destroyed, Jeremiah reminded the people that God would not forget them. God would lead his people back to the Promised Land.

Jeremiah also told them that God would send a wise king to rule them. Jeremiah was talking about Jesus. Jesus is the king of heaven and earth.

God Says He Will Raise Up a King - Jeremiah 23:5

21. EZEKIEL

Like Jeremiah and Isaiah, Ezekiel was a prophet during the Exile.

Ezekiel also spoke about the New Covenant. He told the Israelites that the New Covenant would be a covenant of peace and last forever.

God Promises an Everlatsting Covenant - Ezekiel 37:26

48

Ezekiel told the people many things about God. He said that God would be a Good Shepherd and feed His people.

This came true when Jesus fed the crowd of five thousand people with only five loaves and two fish.

Jesus Feeds the Five Thousand - *Matthew 14:19*

22. JOHN THE BAPTIST

John was called John the Baptist because he would baptize people in the river when they were sorry for their sins.

John the Baptist had a special job. His job was to tell the world that Jesus was coming. He started while he was still in his mother Elizabeth's womb.

When Mary was pregnant with Jesus, she visited Elizabeth. John the Baptist, who was in Elizabeth's womb, leapt for joy when Mary and Jesus arrived.

Mary Visits Elizabeth - Luke 1:39

One day when John was baptizing people in the river, Jesus came to be baptized.

When Jesus was baptized, God sent down a dove and said,

"This is my beloved Son, with whom I am well pleased."

God was telling the world that His son, Jesus, had arrived!

Jesus is Baptized in the Jordan- Matthew 3:13

23. Joseph

Joseph is Jesus' foster-father. An angel appeared to Joseph and told him to take care of Mary and Jesus.

Joseph listened to the angel. Jesus' real Father is God, who is in heaven. Joseph took care of Jesus on earth.

The angel called Joseph a son of David. This was important because God promised that Jesus would be a descendant of King David.

Even though Joseph was Jesus' foster-father, he was related to King David too.

Joseph was a wonderful father and carpenter. He taught Jesus many things.

24. Mary

An angel appeared to Mary and asked if she would be the Mother of God.

Even though this was hard to understand, she had faith in God.

Mary said to the angel, "I am the handmaid of the Lord, let it be done unto me according to thy will." She was saying yes to God.

Gabriel Appears to Mary - Luke 1:26

God kept Mary free from sin. She is the only person other than Jesus who is perfect.

Mary is sometimes called the new Eve. Eve disobeyed God and had to leave the Garden of Eden. But Mary always listened.

Because she said yes to God, Jesus was born on Christmas day.

God Keeps Mary from Sin - *Genesis 3:15*

25. Jesus

We have finally arrived at Christmas, Jesus' birthday.

Even though Jesus is the king of heaven and earth, He came into the world as a poor little boy born in a stable.

Angels came from heaven to announce Jesus' birth. They sang glorious songs to shepherds who came to worship Jesus.

Angels Announce the Birth of Jesus - Luke 2:8

A great star appeared in the sky over the stable. The three wise men followed the star and traveled from faraway lands to come and worship Jesus.

Jesus is called the light of the world like the star that shone brightly in the night.

God kept His promise with Adam and Eve that He would send His Son, Jesus.

When Jesus grew up, He died on the cross for our sins.

Now, all people can go to heaven. This was the final covenant.

All the promises that God made in the Old Testament came true in Jesus' life.

The Magi Come to Worship Jesus
Matthew 2:1

About the Authors

Inspired by the birth of their son Charlie, Theresa and Charles wrote *Bible Characters for Advent* to instill a Christ-centered focus in their Christmas tradition.

They are both alumni of Franciscan University of Steubenville, with a Bachelor of Art in Communications and a Masters in Theology respectively. They live with their son Charlie in Steubenville, Ohio, and both work on campus at Franciscan University.

37642245R10034

Made in the USA
Middletown, DE
03 December 2016